ROOT CE[

FOR PREPPERS

Learn How to Build your Root Cellar to Preserve
Food for the Next 10 Years of Crisis

Tyler Gordon

Table of Contents

INTRODUCTION   8

WHAT EXACTLY IS A ROOT CELLAR?   9

A BRIEF HISTORY OF THE ROOT CELLAR   10

BENEFITS OF HAVING A ROOT CELLAR   12

     Convenience   *13*

     Delicious and Healthy Food   *14*

     Affordability   *14*

     Natural Refrigeration   *15*

CHAPTER 1: CREATING A ROOT CELLAR   16

PLANNING YOUR ROOT CELLAR   16

     Your Needs   *17*

     Your Environment   *18*

     Climatic Conditions   *20*

     Cost   *20*

     Local Authority Permissions   *21*

     Finding the Right Location for Your Root Cellar   *21*

     Plans for Drainage, Airflow, and Lighting   *23*

THE BASICS OF ROOT CELLARING   24

     Humidity   *24*

     Ventilation   *26*

Lighting   28

Temperature   28

DEALING WITH INSECTS AND OTHER COMMON ROOT CELLARING PROBLEMS   30

Rodents   31

Rot   31

Insects   33

Sprouting Vegetables   34

Frozen Produce   35

Produce Going Off Too Quickly   36

Mold   37

CHAPTER 2: WHAT CAN YOU STORE IN A ROOT CELLAR?   **40**

CHAPTER 3: DIFFERENT DESIGN OPTIONS FOR ROOT CELLARS   **46**

EARTH BAG ROOT CELLAR   46

SEPTIC TANK ROOT CELLAR   49

Converting a Septic Tank into a Root Cellar   50

IN-GROUND ROOT CELLAR   52

CONTAINER ROOT CELLAR   57

Zoning   57

Placement   57

Structure   57

Moisture   58

Ventilation   59

THE 'CAVE' CELLAR										59

CHAPTER 4: ROOT CELLAR IN WINTER						**69**

TIPS ON KEEPING YOUR ROOT CELLAR COOL					72

MORE TIPS ON STORAGE AND ROOT CELLAR CONDITIONS			73

CHAPTER 5: STEP-BY-STEP CONSTRUCTION PLAN				**75**

STEP 1: GET A PERMIT									75

STEP 2: CHOOSE A DESIGN								76

STEP 3: ROOT CELLAR PLACEMENT							78

STEP 4: MATERIALS									79

STEP 5: DIGGING IN									81

STEP 6: FOUNDATIONS AND SUPPORT STRUCTURES				82

STEP 7: AN ENTRANCE									85

STEP 8: VENTILATION									86

STEP 9: ELECTRICITY									87

STEP 10: BACKFILLING									87

CHAPTER 6: ROOT CELLAR INTERIOR TIPS AND TRICKS FOR FURNITURE, STORAGE SPACE, AND UTILITIES						**89**

FOOD STORAGE SHELVES								90

Crawlspace										*90*

Plastic Tote										*91*

Under Your Porch									*91*

Window Well in the Basement							*92*

Earth Pit   *92*

Making Use of Cardboard Boxes   *93*

ORGANIZING YOUR SPACE   95

STORING VEGETABLES IN SAND   97

In-Place Storage   *98*

BASIC TIPS   100

CHAPTER 7: HARVESTING, STORING, TRACKING, AND PLANNING   **105**

BEETS   105

BROCCOLI   106

BRUSSELS SPROUTS   107

CABBAGE   108

CARROTS   109

JERUSALEM ARTICHOKES   110

LEEKS   111

PARSNIPS   112

PEARS   113

POTATOES   114

RUTABAGAS   116

TURNIPS   117

WINTER RADISHES   118

ONIONS   118

PUMPKINS   120

SWEET POTATOES   121

TOMATOES   122

CHAPTER 8: YEARLY MAINTENANCE (TIPS, TRICKS, MUST DO, LOG PLAN,

CHECKLIST)   **124**

CLEANING AND SANITIZING A ROOT CELLAR   124

CANNED AND BOTTLED FOODS   129

CONCLUSION   **131**

INTRODUCTION

Learning how to store or preserve food, in general, is critical for anyone attempting to become more self-sufficient, whether for financial, family, health, or disaster reasons. This book will teach you everything you need to know about the humble root cellar, from its origins to modern applications. By the end, you will clearly know what you want to do, how you intend to do it, and when you plan to do it.

You can now store and eat all the fantastic, organic, healthy food you can grow in your garden all year! Forget about the vegetables in the grocery store that are wrapped in dangerous plastic and the expensively imported food that has been sprayed with chemicals. Think about the rows of potatoes and carrots, the corn, the onions, the beets, and all the other produce you may cultivate in your garden and preserve for the winter.

This book will teach you how to build a root cellar from scratch rather than digging one into the ground. After all, not everyone has a large garden and enough space to begin digging a cellar. This book offers some intriguing suggestions that you might find surprising for how to store your vegetables.

What Exactly is a Root Cellar?

Root cellars are technically underground rooms that use the earth's natural humidifying, cooling, and insulating properties. They are a traditional method of storing and preserving food to help people get through the winter. Originally underground rooms, cellars are now any type of storage that preserves food by regulating light, temperature, and humidity. Your refrigerator is the modern root cellar, but if you don't want to rely on electricity, learning how to make a root cellar is essential.

Every root cellar, regardless of design, performs the same basic function. It can keep your food up to 40°F cooler than ambient summertime temperatures if properly constructed. Wintertime benefits of low temperatures include the ability to preserve food longer by preventing rot and deterioration when stored at temperatures slightly above freezing. Even in a basement, the temperatures inside your home are slightly higher, which means stored foods spoil much faster. Most vegetables will become tough, sprout, and spoil if the temperature rises above 45°F.

However, root cellar temperatures vary from one corner to the next. It's important to organize the root cellar effectively because the upper half of the cellar has a temperature that's around 10 degrees warmer than the lower part. Place vegetables that can withstand higher temperatures on top.

What if your garden is too small or you don't want to grow vegetables? No problem—root cellars are intended to store produce that you did not grow yourself. If you can find great deals at your local farm or farmer's market, you can easily store them in your cellar.

A Brief History of the Root Cellar

The root cellar has a fascinating history that dates back at least 40,000 years. Indigenous Australians were the first to use the earth's natural insulation and cooling properties to store food. Records reveal that they developed a means for long-term storage, namely burying it in the ground, more than 40,000 years ago when they were producing enormous quantities of yams. They discovered another process, fermentation, while developing their technique, which is why alcoholic beverages are commonly stored in cellars.

Additionally, underground Iron Age wine cellars that are still used by the Etruscans to keep young wine have been found. The most notable applications of a walk-in root cellar came from English colonists in North America, even though the first alleged use of one was in seventeenth-century England

Ancient China and Egypt had mastered techniques for preserving food, including salting, pickling, utilizing spices, and drying. On the other hand, cold winters and widespread famines drove the British to invent the walk-in root cellar.

Numerous historic root cellars can be found all over eastern Canada and the United States. With more than 135 root cellars, some dating back as far as 200 years, Elliston, a small town in Newfoundland, has even dubbed itself the "Root Cellar Capital of the World".

Benefits of Having A Root Cellar

Root cellaring may sound like an exaggeration, but the effects it could have on your diet and lifestyle would be nothing short of life-changing. This simple, age-old idea of simply burying your food can serve as the foundation for a more sustainable diet and lifestyle, making healthy eating more convenient and affordable.

Let us take a step back for a moment. Before you can decide whether a root cellar is something you should incorporate into your own life, we need to discuss what it is and how it works. A root cellar is simply an underground chamber where food deteriorates much more slowly. The underground environment is ideal for food storage, allowing you to stockpile everything from potatoes to rhubarb wine without using chemicals or canned food.

For millennia, the only way many people could endure winters when no fruits, vegetables, or cereals could grow was by hoarding food in their root cellars. All of that was changed by modern refrigeration, and since the end of World War II, the majority of us have had no trouble, for example, finding strawberries at the grocery store in the middle of February.

Convenience

The beauty of a root cellar is that after you go through the effort of building it, you can have your produce section waiting for you at home, whether you grow your vegetables or buy them from a local farmers market. Yes, a lot of work is involved, but anyone reading this book is unlikely to turn back at the prospect of working up a sweat.

Delicious and Healthy Food

Having your stockpiles of locally grown produce makes it simple to eat healthily. Then, it will take you just as long to stroll to your root cellar, get a few fresh tomatoes and spinach, as it will to prepare something from the freezer that is unnaturally rich in processed flour and fructose. Then, once you've tasted a real tomato, grown naturally, and eaten in season, you'll never return.

Affordability

We've only touched on it so far, but it bears repeating. Every year, storing nutritious food in a root cellar will save you hundreds of dollars in grocery bills. If you grow everything and have a large enough storage capacity, you could save thousands of dollars.

Building your root cellar will need an initial investment, but it will be well worth it in the long run.

Future price increases in food will only be caused by expanding populations and growing fuel costs, as was demonstrated by the dramatic global jump in food prices in 2007 and 2008. We have also seen that eating healthy food costs more money in the United States, Canada, the United Kingdom, and many other Western countries. Paying a premium for healthy living is opposed to the concept of self-sufficiency.

The first step in achieving dietary self-sufficiency is creating a location where you can gather and store all of the natural foods you need; root cellars are made specifically for this purpose. Anyone can build a root cellar with limited construction experience in their spare time or throughout the weekend.

Natural Refrigeration

Despite what the modern world would like you to believe, it is currently possible to live without electric-powered refrigeration. In truth, the solution to long-term food storage and preservation was solved generations ago; it has just been pushed aside by a modern society primarily concerned with instant gratification and a population full of individuals unconcerned with ensuring they have what they need to survive when push comes to shove.

CHAPTER 1: CREATING A ROOT CELLAR

Planning Your Root Cellar

Now begins the most crucial step: making plans for your root cellar. It would be imprudent to run into your backyard and start digging a hole. You must first consider many things to ensure that your root cellar is successful, sustainable, and even scalable.

Your Needs

Why do you think about a root cellar? If you only have a small garden plot that produces a limited number of vegetables, consider the size or style best suits your storage needs.

Suppose you want it to serve as a storm shelter or another emergency shelter. In that case, you'll need to consider construction strength, occupancy capabilities, and storage space for necessities.

Before you even consider root cellar plans, you must first determine what you require from your root cellar. Will it simply be a large underground pantry for farmer's market purchases? Do you have a garden that is producing more and more each year? Do you want to make beer or cider as well? Do you have any young sons who will be teenagers in a few years and who will be able to eat about half of what they weigh each meal? How you answer these questions will determine your capacity needs.

As a general rule, think of an area of 10 feet by 10 feet as being more than enough for storing anything your family could eat. More space might be necessary if you have commercial aspirations or might try home brewing. 5 feet by 8 feet might be adequate for you if you have a small family, a small garden, and you supplement your food supply with weekend trips to the farmers market.

Your Environment

Produce should be stored in cool, humid environments where air can circulate freely. Because the earth is a fantastic temperature regulator, root cellars are typically underground. An ideal climate has a long enough growing season (if you grow your produce) and a cold enough winter to keep the ground below the frost line, no warmer than 50°F (10°C). That encompasses the majority of the populated continent of North America.

For most vegetables, you'll want to create an environment inside your root cellar that approaches the low-40°Fs (5-6°C) because this temperature range prevents them from freezing or sprouting. The ability to maintain this temperature all year is the most important factor in the efficient operation of a root cellar. That means you can't guess the temperature; instead, get a thermometer.

After temperature, you should consider humidity. The ideal humidity range is 70-90%. Much more will spoil your food. It will shrivel if you use less. It is important to note that humidity will fluctuate at different levels within your cellar. A hygrometer is a device that measures humidity, and perfectly useful hygrometers can be purchased online for between $10 and $20.

Your environment should offer you cooler and warmer days according to the season as you'll later be controlling the temperature and humidity of your root cellar with simple air circulation. If you live close to Miami or Fairbanks, Alaska, your climate's extremes don't completely prevent you from having a root cellar, but they do make your job more challenging.

If excavating ground, you must consider what may be below the surface in terms of utility supplies; bursting a water main or an electricity supply can ruin your day. Contact your local utility providers if you have any concerns about previous installations.

Keep an eye out for your local water table or freshwater spring. This can mean that any hole dug into the ground will quickly (or slowly) fill with water. A little damp, however, is perfectly acceptable and essential for a root cellar.

Climatic Conditions

Depending on where you stay, water, cold, and heat will play a different part in your construction details. A cellar in Nevada, for instance, is more likely to be bothered with excess heat than it is to be troubled by water, so waterproofing is maybe not such a big deal – whereby insulation is. And a cellar in Wisconsin has to withstand bitter cold winters to stop the roots from freezing and withstand a fair amount of rainfall. This means more concentration of waterproofing and insulation.

Cost

This is usually a top consideration for most folks and has to be weighed against any advantage gained in the construction.

Consider whether or not a temporary structure would do, even one that you can renew on an annual basis.

Such temporary 'cellars' can be made from straw bales, lumber, or corrugated iron and covered with turf to form a simple yet effective shelter. These shelters are cheap to make and removable at short notice if necessary.

Local Authority Permissions

Something to bear in mind with a more permanent structure is that it may need a building permit or planning permission from your local authority.

This is not usually a problem, especially in rural areas – but better safe than sorry!

Finding the Right Location for Your Root Cellar

This is purely for practical reasons, as trudging through 3 feet of snow to get carrots for dinner is no laughing matter!

If possible, keep it close to the kitchen door, as that is where you will most likely be approaching it (along with the veggie plot).

Your options for location will certainly be limited, especially if you are attaching the root cellar to an existing structure. Here are a few key things to look for in a potential root cellar building site:

- Somewhere higher or elevated so that water runs away from it
- Somewhere away from trees, or specifically tree roots
- Somewhere with no traffic, even if it's just your lawnmower
- Somewhere away from prevailing winds or intense mid-summer sun, possibly on the north face of a hill (south face for anyone in the Southern Hemisphere)

Don't be concerned if your location does not meet these requirements. During the construction and maintenance of your root cellar, you can compensate for any geographical shortcomings.

Also, keep in mind the soil that will surround your cellar. If the terrain is too difficult, you will need professional equipment to locate your location. If the soil is sandy, it may require additional reinforcement or a modified root cellar design. Above all, ensure that the location is sufficiently deep in the earth to allow for proper temperature regulation.

Finally, consider the location's accessibility for yourself. This is a place you will visit daily, so putting it a 10-minute walk from your kitchen or garden would be inconvenient. No problem if your root cellar connects to your basement. However, if you plan to construct your root cellar on a nearby hillside, be ready for a hike through torrential downpours and freezing temperatures. In addition, you will need to clear a path to it in the winter. An inconvenient root cellar would miss the point entirely.

Plans for Drainage, Airflow, and Lighting

As mentioned before, drainage and airflow will play key roles in the maintenance of your root cellar. In the future, we'll talk about the supplies you'll need to correctly drain the water from your root cellar, but for now, just know that you'll need to take this into account. The same holds true for ventilation and airflow. You'll need to make a route for fresh air to enter the room while keeping vermin and other animals out.

The Basics of Root Cellaring

Humidity

Root cellars require high humidity levels of 85-95%. This prevents your stored produce from drying out and becoming shriveled. There are three ways to achieve the right levels of humidity in your root cellar:

- **A Dirt Floor:** Dirt floors retain moisture much more easily than concrete or stone floors. Assume you dug a root cellar into the ground. You already have an advantage in that case because the soil will provide some humidity. The earth should be packed in tightly, followed by a layer of gravel. This serves two purposes: it keeps your feet dry when things get wet and aids in moisture retention. If your cellar becomes dry, spray some water (carefully) over the gravel. Water evaporates quickly, adding moisture and humidity to the air.

- **Adding Water:** There are other options if you do not want to add gravel or if your floors are made of concrete. You can add water by lightly spraying the floor, spreading damp burlap bags over the vegetables (but not soaking them), or placing a few water pans on the floor. These measurements are usually required in the fall when you first put your produce into storage. Dug-in root cellars are less likely to require humidity assistance than basement root cellars. In areas where the air is very moist, keep root vegetables in uncovered bins to keep them firm and smooth.

If your humidity falls below optimal levels, there is a third option: sawdust, moss, or sand. You can pack your fruits and vegetables with damp sawdust, moss, or sand. This is especially effective for parsnips, beets, and carrots, as it reduces surface evaporation.

One of the most critical considerations is that warm air absorbs more moisture than cool air. The environment will be somewhat unstable if your root cellar is damp and cold. If your air temperature is 34°F, it has room to absorb a little more moisture. If the temperature falls a few degrees, the air will become saturated. The "dew point" is the temperature at which the air can no longer hold excess moisture. This water will condense on your ceiling, walls, and fruits and vegetables. The most secure way to ensure your humidity levels are correct is to purchase a hygrometer, which can be found at any hardware store or garden center.

Ventilation

Each root cellar is unique and will necessitate its methods of regulating ventilation and humidity. The most important thing to keep an eye on is the conditions inside your root cellar, and make sure you can change your design if necessary, preferably before you start building.

Alternatively, make sure your design allows for changes to be made later.

The simplest way to vent your cellar is with two 3- to 4-inch-wide vents. To ensure proper air circulation, place the first near the ceiling and the second near the floor.

Proper ventilation is just as important as humidity. Air must be allowed to enter and circulate through the cellar to keep the temperature low. Adjusting the air intake is critical for reducing extra humidity and preventing condensation from ruining your hard work. When air circulates effectively, ethylene gas from some fruits and other vegetable odors that could change the flavors of other fruits and vegetables are eliminated.

Understanding how air circulates through your root cellar necessitates recalling basic physics—hot air rises (lighter) and cold air falls (heavier). A large or enclosed cellar requires an air intake system and an air outlet. The intake should be low in the room to bring cool air from outside. The outlet should be elevated to allow warmer air to escape. To allow for efficient air circulation, place the outlet and inlet on opposite sides of the room.

If your storage area is small or there are many cracks allowing air in (think old stone foundations), you may only need one high-up outlet to remove the warm air. Keep it a couple of inches above the ground when storing your produce to allow air to circulate beneath it.

Lighting

Finally, consider the lighting in your cellar. A root cellar should essentially be as dark as possible—too much light can cause rotting and sprouting. Have a single light bulb in your cellar, but don't leave it on for any longer than necessary. You can also use burlap to keep the light out while allowing for adequate air circulation and ventilation. Cover any windows that you use for ventilation with dark material.

Temperature

Temperature is the most critical variable to consider in a root cellar. A good root cellar does two things: it borrows cold and keeps it cold. How do you borrow when it's cold? It's simple: dig a hole in the ground. The earth will remain at a temperature of around 52 degrees below the frost line.

This is because the deeper earth temperature is less affected by freezing temperatures above, providing your vegetables with more protection. If you don't want to dig your root cellar into the ground, you can borrow the cold through a window or an exhaust pipe that you can close off. These options allow cold night air into the cellar but should be turned off during the day as temperatures rise.

Maintaining a temperature range of 32-40°F is ideal for food storage. You can still use the root cellar as a short-term storage area for apples and root vegetables if your temperatures are between 40°F and 50°F. Tomatoes, peppers, and eggplant can be stored for about a month.

You must invest in a good thermometer to monitor your root cellar temperatures.

Dealing with Insects and Other Common Root Cellaring Problems

If your cellar is appropriately sealed at all joints and vulnerable points, pests should not be a problem. However, the constant opening of the door will eventually let an unwanted guest in. We recommend simply using whatever pest-control methods you use in your house for your cellar. If you use mouse traps, put one or two in your cellar. If you use dryer sheets or spices to keep ants out of entry points, do the same for your cellar. Regular maintenance should be enough to keep your cellar free of pests.

Rodents

Mice and rats can be found anywhere there is food, including root cellars. The key to keeping them out is to prevent them from entering your root cellar in the first place, and the simplest way to do so is to seal off their entry points. Metal wire mesh is one of the best options for this. Place it over any entry points for these creatures, including vents. Consider elevating your storage if you're having trouble keeping mice out of your cellar. Remember that many rodents can climb; if their prize is your food, they will go to any length to get it. We'll look at some natural ways to keep rodents and other pests out of your root cellar later, but for now, keep it clean. You should also think about putting traps along the walls, which should be checked at least once a day and any dead rodents removed immediately.

Rot

Rot is an unavoidable problem in root cellars. You've probably heard the expression "one rotten apple spoils the barrel," which couldn't be truer. But how do you prevent this from happening? You cannot entirely prevent it, but you can significantly reduce its occurrence.

Take extra care when harvesting your vegetables. Before storing your produce, go through it and set aside anything damaged during the harvest, such as a fork cut or a space.

Set aside anything that has been bruised. If you drop something, such as an apple or a potato, it will almost certainly have an invisible bruise, even if it does not appear damaged. Set it aside, too.

Only foods that are undamaged and free of blemishes should be stored in your root cellar. Those damaged can be used immediately or stored in another way, such as freezing or canning.

Another common mistake is washing root vegetables before storing them—do not do this, no matter how tempting it may be. Root vegetables store much better when harvested with intact roots, stems, and soil. Washing vegetables removes moisture from them, hastening their decomposition.

Make sure that any canned or bottled foods have airtight lids. Before canning or bottling anything, the containers and lids must be sterilized—even the smallest amount of contamination can spoil the contents.

When storing produce, place the largest items at the back and the smallest items first—these are more likely to spoil quickly and should be used as soon as possible.

Check for condensation if your cellar is humid. When water drips from the ceiling or down the walls, it can get onto your produce and cause it to rot. Pretreat your cellar ceiling with a disinfectant, such as chlorine, before storing your food, as this slows the spread of diseases caused by dripping water.

As a cardinal rule, check your root cellar regularly. Any foods starting to wither, rot, or show signs of decomposition should be removed immediately.

Insects

This seems to be more of a problem where nuts and grains are stored, and since you have other food in your root cellar, you should never use chemical sprays or insecticides. The best way to keep insects out of your root cellar is to have a tight-fitting door, all cracks sealed up, and insect mesh over the vents and drainage.

Alternatively, you can scatter bay leaves around—insects hate these with a passion—or other herbs with a strong smell.

Sprouting Vegetables

If you notice your root cellar vegetables sprouting, it means something is wrong, and it usually boils down to one of three things:

- **Ethylene Gas**: Look where you've stored the sprouting vegetables. What other ethylene-producing fruits and vegetables are nearby? If so, relocate them. Inspect your ventilation system as well—is it adequate? Is it functional? Is it in the correct location? If you answered "no" to any or all of these, it's a sign that something in your cellar needs to be adjusted.

- **Too Hot**: If the temperature is too high, it can force vegetables to grow, which you don't want in your cellar. When a plant begins to grow again, it must be consumed quickly. Check your ventilation system once more to prevent any more sprouting.

- **Too Much Light**: Do you visit your root cellar with the door open? Are the windows draped? Do you leave a light on for extended periods? The only way to prevent vegetables from growing again is to keep them as dark as possible.

Frozen Produce

If your root cellar produce is freezing, it simply means that the temperature is far too low. Check your thermometer first. If the temperature is below freezing, it must be raised. However, at this point, you may have already lost a significant portion of your stored foods. When most vegetable freeze, they become mushy and rot, rendering them useless. The second thing to look for is which vegetables have been frozen. If only those at the bottom are affected, the air coming in through the inlet is too cold, indicating that you did not dig your root cellar deep enough. There isn't much you can do about it except empty it and dig deeper. Remember that constant temperature stability is achieved at approximately ten feet or three meters underground.

Produce Going Off Too Quickly

Have you ever opened the door to your root cellar and been taken aback by the smell? Yes, your food is spoiling quickly, and the odor is strong. So, what would cause that to occur? Simply put, the climate in your root cellar is to blame. The main culprits are moisture, light, air, temperature, and microbial growth.

Damage caused by microorganisms such as yeast, mold, and bacteria is one of the most common causes of fresh food spoilage. However, this can only occur if the conditions are favorable—they require nutrients and water to grow and reproduce. Most fruits and vegetables have an average water content of 90%, making them an ideal target.

Light is a major adversary of fresh food in storage. Excessive exposure will cause the outer layer of the vegetable or fruit to spoil. This is known as photodegradation, and it causes discoloration as well as the loss of flavor, proteins, and vitamins.

The only thing you should never do is store vegetables or fruits wet or in an airtight container. A lack of air circulation does nothing but hasten decay. Water will pool on the produce if your humidity levels are too high, causing it to rot again.

Finally, the temperature is an important consideration that must be met. Keep in mind that some vegetables prefer it cool, while others prefer it hot. Temperature extremes can be problematic—cold to the point of freezing causes the food to form ice crystals inside, which expand and break through the cell walls, causing discoloration and, in some cases, a slimy texture.

One of the most important things to do is get your climate right on point before you start storing food. Once your cellar is full, use your thermometer and hygrometer to measure temperature and humidity. Using a notebook to record your results daily can give you an early warning when something is wrong.

Mold

When your root cellar is functioning properly, it will be cool all year, and the humidity level will be consistent. On the other hand, mold can affect all root cellars, whether underground, in a basement or garage, under the porch, or on a simple barrel in the ground. While you may believe you have properly sealed your cellar, construction flaws or inadequate maintenance can lead to mold growing in places you do not want.

Mold growth in your root cellar can harm the air you breathe if it is attached to or inside your home. Condensation is the cause of mold growth in a cellar or cold storage. It could be due to warmer air seeping into the room during the summer months, which happens when the door is not sealed correctly.

Condensation forms when warm air meets cold surfaces in your cellar, such as the roof or poorly insulated walls. This creates ideal conditions for mold to grow. That mold will quickly spread to your produce or onto the containers where your food is stored, and within a few days, your entire crop will be ruined—that is how quickly it can happen.

Your root cellar should have air vents, one of the best tools for controlling humidity. As a result, you can better control the environment and prevent mold growth—these air vents will keep fresh air moving through your cellar and keep it dry.

However, mold does not come from only one source. You can introduce it into your cellar through the food you bring in. No matter how well your root cellar works, the mold will grow and spread to other foods and the root cellar structure.

If you suspect or see mold growing in your root cellar, you need to do something about it immediately. If left unchecked, mold can quickly spread to other areas, especially if your root cellar is attached to your home. Professional help will be needed to remove the mold and repair the damage already done in some cases.

CHAPTER 2: WHAT CAN YOU STORE IN A ROOT CELLAR?

Because different vegetables have varying degrees of sensitivity, some will require more attention than others. Potatoes require little care and can be stored in a cellar for months at a time. Less hardy vegetables, such as tomatoes or apples, require frequent inspection and discarding any bad ones.

You can also keep cured meats and cheeses in the cellar, depending on the conditions you create.

While the temperature and humidity in your root cellar are ideal for vegetables and some fruits, metal containers should not be stored there. It will rust and spoil if you store canned food or anything with a metal lid in your cellar for an extended period. The same is true for flour, oatmeal, and any other cereal that needs to be kept dry. A root cellar is simply too humid for any food that absorbs moisture easily.

Having a root cellar allows you to enjoy vegetables and fruits that are out of season or produce that is not available at the grocery store unless sprayed and imported. You don't have to bottle, can, boil, or freeze anything to accomplish this.

Furthermore, you will no longer be limited to storing only certain vegetables—carrots, potatoes, and turnips. You can store nuts, fresh tomatoes, cantaloupes, sweet potatoes, and more if you carefully plan your root cellar program.

Don't worry if you find that you can't always fill your root cellar with what you grow. Visit the farmer's markets and purchase in-season or storage vegetables in the fall.

Here are some of the foods you can store along with useful indications:

Food	Temperature	Humidity	Shelf-Life
Apples	32°F	90 to 95%	Two to seven months, depending on the variety
Dried Beans	50 to 60°F	60 to 70%	One year
Beets	32°F	90 to 95%	Three to five months
Broccoli	32°F	90 to 95%	One to two weeks
Brussels Sprouts	32°F	90 to 95%	Three to five weeks
Cabbage	32°F	90 to 95%	Three to four months

Carrots	32°F	90 to 95%	Four to six months
Garlic	50 to 60°F	60 to 70%	Five to eight months
Jerusalem Artichokes	32°F	90 to 95%	One to two months
Leeks	32°F	90 to 95%	Three to four months
Onions	50 to 60°F	60 to 70%	Five to eight months
Parsnips	32°F	90 to 95%	One to two months
Pears	30°F	90 to 95%	Two to three months
Potatoes	40 to 45°F	90 to 95%	Four to six months

Pumpkins	50 to 60°F	60 to 70%	Five to six months
Rutabagas	32°F	90 to 95%	Two to four months
Squash	50 to 60°F	60 to 70%	Four to six months
Sweet Potatoes	55 to 60°F	60 to 70%	Four to six months
Tomatillos	50 to 60°F	60 to 70%	One to two months
Tomatoes	50 to 60°F	60 to 70%	One to two months—green tomatoes Four to six months for those varieties bred for winter storage
Turnips	32°F	90 to 95%	Four to six months

The above list gives you an idea of the temperatures and humidity levels at which certain foods must be stored.

As established, root cellars can be used to store just about anything these days. Traditionally, they were used to store root vegetables, mainly potatoes, turnips, and carrots. Today, people store other root vegetables, apples, pears, hard fruits, *etc.* In addition, you can store canned foods, medicines, salted meat and fish, and so much more. If you build one big enough, you can use it as an emergency shelter!

This will ensure that your food supplies last as long as possible without spoiling and losing flavor or nutritional value. Typically, you will have some food that needs to be stored in damp, cold environments and others that need a drier and warmer environment. In the list below, the produce has been sorted according to its temperature requirements, providing information on how to harvest and store it, along with a few good storage varieties.

All the fruits and vegetables listed must be stored at 32-40°F and 90-95% humidity.

CHAPTER 3: DIFFERENT DESIGN OPTIONS FOR ROOT CELLARS

Earth Bag Root Cellar

This root cellar design is ideal for building into a hill or the ground and will save a significant amount of money on construction materials because it is built using earth bags, sturdy bags that come in various sizes and are then simply filled with dirt, as the name implies. The first step in this design is selecting the appropriate earth bags for your project.

Filling the earth bags is a laborious process made much easier with at least two people. One person should be in charge of filling the bags with usable dirt that is free of vegetation and stones and packed tightly, and another should take the filled bags and position them.

What You Require:

- Earthenware bags
- Door/window frames made of wood
- Gravel
- Barbed wire
- Baling Twine for PVC Pipe

What You Should Do:

1. Make room for at least an 8x8 rounded root cellar.
2. Drainage for the root cellar should be laid out using a 4-inch PVC pipe perforated to allow for proper drainage. Drainage will be adequate if the pipe is laid on a 4% grade down and out of the space.
3. Place one foot of gravel on top of the pipe and firmly tamp it down; this will be the root cellar's floor.
4. This earth bag root cellar will be perfectly round, as each ring of earth bags has a smaller diameter than

the previous one until it closes at the top. To determine the starting point, use a compass and ruler to take precise measurements.

5. Remove the door frame and decide where you want the ventilation to go.

6. Lay out the first level of earth bags, considering the doorway and additional walkways. To give the earth bags some extra weight, the first few levels should be filled with 20% concrete and 80% dirt. The remainder can be filled with dirt alone.

7. After that, each layer of bags must be tamped down and covered in two lengths of barbed wire across the course.

   Each layer of bags should naturally move closer to the center of the root cellar, resulting in each layer taking up less space. Do not rush this process because allowing it to happen naturally will result in a structure as solid as any traditionally built structure.

   If done correctly, your buttress walls will be little more than earth bags connected to the main structure at the door frame.

8. Fill in the rest of the displaced dirt around the structure with at least two layers of polyethylene.

9. Cover the inside with lime plaster to allow the walls to "breathe," which will act as a moisture barrier.

10. Consider shelving carefully as round root cellars tend to have less space, allowing each shelf a bit of breathing room.

Septic Tank Root Cellar

This root cellar design splits the difference between the first two by taking a prefabricated item and burying it outside. Remember, only an unused septic tank would be appropriate for storing food. A great way to find a cheap future root cellar for cheap is to find septic tank whole sellers in your area and see if they are willing to sell any tanks they have which might have defects rendering them unusable for their intended purpose.

A 1500-gallon tank averages about five and a half feet wide, tall, and ten feet long, while a 2500-gallon tank provides an extra foot of headroom. New undamaged 2500-gallon tanks cost around $1600, while otherwise unusable tanks cost about half that. When buying a tank, ask the seller to remove the partition that is almost certainly inside, though it can be punched through manually if necessary.

Converting a Septic Tank into a Root Cellar

Once you've located a septic tank and dug out a location for it, it's time to spread a layer of crushed stone beneath the final resting place to support what's to come. Ensure that your layer of stone will keep the tank level once it is in place.

After the tank has been installed, it is time to construct a door and ventilation points. This is most easily accomplished with a concrete-cutoff saw. Begin by marking a four-inch spot four inches from the bottom of the tank on the side facing out of the hole that does not have an effluent pipe hole. This is the bottom of your door.

Cut out the space for the door and ventilation holes with a concrete-cutoff saw, wearing eye and ear protection. As needed, use a sledgehammer.

You can build your door, but getting it to seal is difficult; instead, consider an insulated steel door in a pre-hung frame. Before you cut the hole, look for a door.

When cutting vent holes, ensure they are at least four inches in diameter. Because the effluent pipe hole is already a four-inch hole leading out of the tank's top, you will likely only need to cut an entry air hole and use that for the exit pipe. Make an additional drainage hole in the center of the tank at the bottom for easy cleaning.

All that is left is to fill in the hole where your new root cellar sits. Before you do that, however, be sure to seal the access hatch at the top of the tank. Next, cover the top of the tank with a few layers of polyethylene to ensure the roof is waterproof.

Once the tank is buried, construct a retaining wall at the doorway to prevent dirt from getting inside.

In-Ground Root Cellar

Building an underground root cellar takes a lot of time and commitment, so if you don't have either, you should look into another type of root cellar. If you are not skilled at construction or do not have the necessary tools, consider hiring a professional contractor to assist you.

First and foremost, you must select the materials from which your root cellar will be constructed. Among the options are:

- Natural stone
- Block of cinder/concrete
- Logs of cedar
- Tires stacked with dirt

Most people prefer cinder blocks because they are inexpensive and readily available in most builders' yards or DIY stores.

You could use a fiberglass water tank if you want to take a different approach and let your creative side run wild. These are easily adaptable to your needs and are easier to bury than digging out an entire room and constructing walls. Simply ensure that it is well-ventilated and has at least one foot of soil.

Consider your flooring options for the in-ground root cellar. Most people lay concrete, flat stones, or a packed earth floor with a layer of gravel. This is the cheapest and often best option because it ensures humidity can be better controlled.

Take into account the location of your root cellar. It must be located in a well-drained area—the last thing you want is water running in. You must also consider the water table; an in-ground root cellar cannot be built where the water table is high. Finally, ensure the opening faces north to limit exposure to the hot sun during the day. Consider ventilation, temperature, and humidity wherever your root cellar is located.

The first step to constructing your root cellar is making a hole. Depending on the size of your root cellar, you may need to use a backhoe or hire a contractor who owns one to assist you in digging it.

Dig deeper for footings around the cellar, then pour in the concrete. You must now wait at least twenty-four to forty-eight hours for this to harden.

When the concrete has hardened, you can start constructing your walls. Take your time with this step— it's a big job, and attempting to lay all the bricks at once will lead to disaster. Again, if you are not confident in your bricklaying abilities, consider hiring someone to do it for you.

You should also check your ventilation at this point. A 3 to 4 inches diameter PVC pipe should be inserted at the cellar's bottom to draw in colder air. A second one of the same size must be installed near the top to vent the hot air and ethylene gas. Ensure your vent pipes are covered with breathable screens so air can flow while keeping pests out.

Frame your entrance as you build the wall. After all, you'll need a way in! Build the footings for the door five brick rows high.

Make your roof. You could pour a flat concrete slab for the top, but condensation would be a major issue. As a result, the best option is to construct an arched roof. This necessitates excellent carpentry skills (or hiring someone to do the job for you!).

To build a strong enough structure, you will need 12-inch plywood and 2x4s; it will need to be built, disassembled, and reassembled on your cellar walls.

First, construct your skeleton out of 2x4s and plywood, as shown below:

Next, cover the roof of your structure with plywood.

Put it back together on the cellar walls.

Before covering the entire roof with rebar, place the plywood cover on top, cover it with a tight plastic sheet, and affix it to the structure.

Pour your concrete now. It should be 6 inches thick and cover the entire structure and the wall bricks. Unless you have a contractor on hand, you will most likely need to do this in sections.

Now is the time to be patient! Before removing the wooden form from the inside, the concrete must cure and dry. Allow two to three days before attempting to remove the form. A waterproof sealant should also be brushed over the concrete.

The next step is to construct your stairs. This is best done with concrete, though wooden ones can be built if desired. Add a top and bottom door, and your root cellar is complete.

Two doors are recommended because they keep creatures out and cooler air in—just remember to close the top door before opening the bottom one. You'll also need light atop the stairs to see your way down.

If you want to keep your cellar floor as packed earth, you can layer gravel on top of it.

To organize your cellar, use wooden shelves on your walls; these are not so fast to conduct heat and cold and can help you regulate your temperatures.

Container Root Cellar

Zoning

Before you can even think of using a steel container as a root cellar, you need to check if any zoning laws (city, county, or state) stop you from doing it or restrict where or how you do it.

Placement

Chances are you already decided this when you checked out the zoning laws. When you decide this, think carefully about how you will use your container. If you build it into a hill, you will want a door and steps to access it.

Structure

If you choose to bury your container, you need to think carefully about how it will stand the pressure on it from the earth. Containers are not exactly designed to be buried; they were designed to be stacked on a ship or at the docks. The only load-bearing parts of a container are the four corner posts—the sides are strong enough to support the roof, and that is it. You may need to plan on erecting a retaining wall around where your container is located without forgetting to include drainage. If you do, heavy downpours could submerge your container, fully or partially. If you are entirely burying your container, you will need a platform that pushes the earth's weight onto the four corner posts. The one thing you should never do is dig your hole and bury the container without planning—it will most certainly collapse.

Moisture

While containers are watertight and windproof, you need to consider how you will stop the earth's moisture from getting in. The floor is built of steel cross-members with treated plywood on top. You need to think about sealing underneath the floor and possibly pouring a cement base first. Your container must also be sealed with plastic tarps, roofing tar, or truck bed liners. Do your research and find the most cost-effective way of sealing your container for optimum results.

Ventilation

Your container cellar must have good ventilation and air circulation; otherwise, anything you store in it will be destroyed. The principle here is the same as any other type of root cellar.

Once your container root cellar is in place, you can follow the same rules for any type of root cellar. You can add an extra door and use it as a storm shelter—at least it will have food!

The 'Cave' Cellar

The term 'cave' simply comes from the fact that it is usually built into a sloping hillside, leaving only the front entrance visible. The rest of the building is covered with soil to a depth of at least 36 inches over the roof.

Of course, there are times when it takes up residence in a cave, with some modifications to make it fit for its purpose.

This is undoubtedly the most expensive type of root cellar (unless you have a cave!), and, of course, it depends on you having a hillside to build it into. A similar type, however, can be built by utilizing a dip in the ground to minimize excavation.

Depending on your specific circumstances, it can also be built on level ground and hidden beneath a mound of soil.

An early example of an old Root Cellar is one dug into a hillside and turfed over.

Depending on ground conditions, permanency, and other factors, there are numerous ways to build a cave-style root cellar.

The materials used can range from concrete blocks to lumber to straw bales! A temporary cellar can be built with straw bale walls and a strong timber roof to hold a few inches of soil or sod to insulate it.

However, in this case, we will look at a permanent structure that involves building into the hillside. However, the same construction methods can be used in various situations.

Caution: Imagination is required!

Material List (15 feet by 8 feet by 8 feet):

- Concrete block (CMU) 16 x 9 x 8 - 390 blocks
- 1.5 cubic yards of pre-mixed concrete for footings
- 2.15 cubic yards of pre-mixed roof concrete
- 4 - 8x4 insulating roof sheets (choose thickness), sand, and cement for mortar
- Rear vent pipe (minimum 4") long enough to reach from the floor to the finished ground level
- Front door, window (if applicable), and vent pipe
- Rough sand or gravel for the inside base
- Screws and fasteners

Note: These are all estimated measurements.

Construction Procedures:

- Step 1 - Equipment: Unless you intend to work on it for months or years, hire a backhoe and a driver. This is back-breaking work to do by hand.

- Step 2 - Digging: Dig into the hillside 18 feet deep by 13 feet wide for a cellar 15 feet deep by 8 feet wide by 8 feet high (internal). This is to allow for the width of the two walls to be 16 inches and access around the construction to apply a damp-proof membrane before backfilling.

- Step 3 - Foundations: Measure the internal width of the cellar, then mark and dig out a foundation area that is the center of the walls, as shown in the diagram below.

- Step 4 - Walls: After pouring the foundations and allowing them to set, build the walls with concrete blocks according to the diagram, and let them set for two days or so.

- Step 5 - Roof: Keep in mind that the roof is load-bearing and thus must be both strong and waterproof. This is accomplished by building a framework of 4x2 timbers topped by a 34-inch ply board.

The timbers are secured to the inside of the wall with appropriate wall screws or nails. The 4 x 2 timbers are spaced at 24-inch intervals, just like you would when building a floor.

This will support the concrete while it sets and will be left in place to form the cellar ceiling - minus the vertical supports, which will be knocked away once the concrete has fully cured.

A vent pipe, consisting of one 4-inch pipe at the back of the cellar, leading from the floor level up through the roof, must be installed before this stage. Fit insect mesh to the outside cap to keep flies and bugs away.

A second vent will be installed on the front wall near the ceiling level to allow warm air to escape and create an air flow.

The reinforcing steel mesh is then laid on 'lifts' of stone or slate so that it is roughly in the center of the concrete when it is poured.

The timberwork has been shuttered at 6 inches high, allowing the poured concrete to cover the wall head completely.

The plywood extends to the inside edge, level with the wall head.

Tip: If you use concrete blocks without reinforcing the walls, the tops can be covered with slate or other material to keep the concrete from pouring down the inside cavity.

Before pouring concrete, a polythene sheet is laid over the timber in the preceding example. This is a good precaution because it prevents water from soaking into the woodwork below. This water-logged wood can cause the concrete to dry out too quickly, leading to mold growth later on.

The Damp-Proof Membrane (DPM) completely covers the roof and walls. This can be a polythene membrane or a good tar-based coating, especially on the walls - follow the manufacturer's application instructions.

I prefer to cover the roof area with a high-quality pond liner, such as EPDM. This is very flexible, will not tear easily, and is reasonably priced for the roof area (it should cost less than $100).

Make sure that the membrane is tucked OVER the membrane on the walls. This ensures that the joint is waterproof.

- Step 6 - Front Door: I have assumed up to this point that you are aware of the need for a front door. Yes? Good! How difficult can it be to build a wall with a door?

Although this is 'good enough,' it can be improved by including a second door inside the first - even if it is at the end of a short corridor. This improves the insulative qualities and is a great barrier against heat and cold when you access your cellar.

In addition, a 2-inch builder insulating board on the inside of the door and front wall area, which are the only areas exposed to the elements, is an excellent idea for insulation.

- Step 7 - Infilling: Before filling the area to the side of the cellar, protect your DPM with a thin fiberboard to prevent it from being torn.

Depending on whether you have enough roof covering, the roof is covered with 2–4-inch builders insulating board at this stage (at least 3 feet of soil). While covering over with earth will insulate your cellar and protect the DPM.

- Step 8 – Cellar Interior: Because your root cellar must have high relative humidity, no attempt is made to prevent ALL water from entering.

For example, the floor is best finished with fine gravel or sand over the dirt itself. In most cases, this should provide just the right amount of moisture.

If timber racking is used, some people prefer to run a border of concrete or slabs around the edge for the legs to stand, leaving only a 4-foot-wide channel of gravel down the center.

A Front Vent (4-inch pipe) must be installed on the front wall, high up near the ceiling. This allows warmer air to escape while the rear vent draws in cooler air, resulting in an ideal air flow in your Cellar.

If possible, an opening window should be included in the front wall construction to allow for better air flow when conditions call for it.

As previously stated, humidity is essential in your roof cellar because it prevents the vegetables from drying out and wrinkling. However, too much water can cause other issues, such as moldy vegetables and walls, which is not good.

The loose-fill flooring should provide enough natural humidity to meet your needs; if not, keep some water in an open trough or basin to help with humidity levels.

However, if the ground water rises during heavy rainfall and your cellar becomes inundated, you may need to install a lift pump in a suitable location.

This is more of an issue in a basement cellar or another cellar buried below ground level.

When the water level rises, a floatation switch in the pump activates automatically, clearing away the water before it becomes a problem.

It only requires a suitable hole dug in the floor and lined with brick or concrete – a sunken barrel or bucket will suffice. This should be at the bottom of a slope so that any water that falls on it is directed to it, possibly with the help of a simple gutter.

When the hole begins to fill, the pump is activated, and the water is pumped to the location you specify.

A perforated barrel is another option. Make the hole larger than the barrel and fill the surrounding space with pea gravel. If the water table is a problem, this will collect water seepage from the surrounding soil.

Keep this in mind when selecting building materials and consider using heavy timber in dry climates where wood rot is less of an issue (timber is an excellent insulator).

Excess water affects the damp-proofing methods used to protect the structure and the measures required to prevent mold in wet climates.

CHAPTER 4: ROOT CELLAR IN WINTER

Depending on your physical location, your root cellar may be predisposed more towards one type of produce or storage method than the others. Suppose the area you live in is known for having mild winters. In that case, it may not be possible to get the low temperatures required for storing fruits and vegetables, and the most you might be able to get away with is storing things like grains, nuts, and dried fruit, much the way the ancient Egyptians did.

On the other hand, if the area where you are building your root cellar is known to be extremely cold, then your main goal will be to keep what you have stored from freezing. Cold-weather root cellars typically need extra layers of insulation and constructed air vents so that the sun warms the air as it travels down. Large barrels of water or a few hanging light bulbs powered by a generator can also keep the space warm.

In most places, root cellars will likely not be listed among the types of projects requiring permits. Unfortunately, this is mainly because they have fallen out of fashion, not because they do not require any sort of permit. This is occasionally not the case in predominantly rural areas where they are considered sheds for storing agriculture and exempt from regulation. Several other types of additional construction can also require additional permits. These include:

For a root shelter, the general idea is to create a cool space where the temperature stays at 32-40°F (0-4.4 C) with a humidity level of between 85-95%.

The reason for the cool temperature is that it slows the release of ethylene gas and stops microorganisms from growing, which causes the vegetables to decompose.

The humidity level is crucial because it stops your vegetables from drying out through evaporation, leading to withered-looking veggies!

This is the ideal temperature and humidity level to store a range of root vegetables, such as carrots, turnips, beets, parsnips, potatoes, and many other vegetables throughout the winter.

Ventilation is another important consideration for a successful root cellar. It removes excess water or condensation and replenishes the oxygen supply keeping the area fresh and reducing the chances of mold.

However, do not be fooled into thinking that a root cellar is only for winter use! During hot summer, the cooler interior of your root cellar will also double up as a free-to-use (no electric bills) temporary storage area for most kinds of vegetables and other food products.

Though not as cold as your refrigerator, it will keep most vegetables fresh and free-up the fridge for items such as dairy products – depending on your local weather conditions.

Tips on Keeping Your Root Cellar Cool

You must consider these aspects to store your vegetables effectively over the winter months. Creating the optimum atmosphere can be done by following these simple tips:

- Your root cellar should be dug about ten feet (or three meters), where temperature stability is reached.
- Do not site a dug-in root cellar near large trees. Not only will you find digging through the roots challenging, but they will eventually grow through your cellar walls.
- Use wooden platforms, bins, and shelves to store your produce on and in. Wood does not conduct the cold or heat as quickly as metal does, and plastic may turn brittle.

- Ensure your shelves are between 1 and 3 inches from the walls—this ensures good air circulation, minimizing the chances of airborne mold.
- If your root cellar is outdoors, the best flooring is packed earth, whereas, in a basement cellar, concrete is more practical and works better.
- Make sure you have a handy hygrometer and thermometer and check them daily.
- Use inlets and outlets to regulate heat and cold into and out of the root cellar.

More Tips on Storage and Root Cellar Conditions

If you need to preserve moisture in your cellar and create a humid microclimate, place the vegetables that need that climate in individual bags with holes. Alternatively, you can use perforated, sealed plastic containers. Avoid regular plastic containers—although they do work for some things.

On the other hand, dry microclimates can be created using sealed containers containing moisture-absorbing materials. A cup of rice, for example, absorbs air moisture while keeping the rice away from your vegetables.

Begin planning your root cellar storage as soon as the planting season begins. Choose varieties designed for long-term storage.

When harvesting vegetables, avoid washing them before storing them. The cellar will be disease-fighting, and washing it off may be harmful.

Do your homework—some vegetables must be cured before storing, while others store better if exposed to frost. Proper research ensures that your produce has the longest possible shelf life.

Nothing diseased or damaged should be stored. If you bruise or cut any vegetable or fruit while harvesting, set it aside—it should be eaten first.

Check your storage every couple of weeks to ensure nothing is going bad. If anything is, get rid of it right away before it ruins the rest of your harvest.

CHAPTER 5: STEP-BY-STEP CONSTRUCTION PLAN

Step 1: Get a Permit

Building permits are required in most US states for any new construction, including root cellars. Permits are typically issued at the county or local level, so get in touch with your local governing body.

In addition, zoning regulations or neighborhood uniformity laws may place restrictions on where and how you can construct your root cellar. It is critical to conduct all of this due diligence ahead of time, well before you begin digging, to avoid fines or other penalties.

If you must get some food into the ground and don't have time to consider a proper design fully, a metal garbage can buried in the ground can provide you with a temporary refuge.

Begin by digging a hole slightly larger than the diameter of the can and deep enough to allow the can to sit about four inches below the soil line.

Place the garbage can in the hole and fill the space around it with excess straw to insulate it. When you're finished, replace the lid, wrap it in plastic, and add more straw or mulch to help the contents maintain a consistent temperature.

This method works well for storing root vegetables especially, and they will keep in this fashion all winter long

Step 2: Choose a Design

While the traditional root cellar dug into the side of a hill may still be suitable for some, most modern root cellars are built straight down with stairs eventually leading down to the door. Colder climates will almost certainly necessitate the installation of a second door as a form of extra insulation. Root cellars have also been built using metal culverts or simple materials such as barrels, packing crates, or pallets to store an underground cache of food and supplies.

Regardless of style, the true value of any root cellar is the extra insulation it receives from the soil surrounding it. One foot underground can provide a temperature drop of up to 20 degrees compared to summertime temperatures above ground. A minimum of three or four feet of soil above the top of your root cellar is required to make it worthwhile, and a full ten feet of dirt between your root cellar and the outside world (both above and on either side) allows for the most insulation and temperature control. Remember, to get the most out of your root cellar, keep the temperature between 32°F and 40°F and the humidity between 70% and 85%. Temperatures up to 50°F can also be effective, though anything above that will not significantly slow the rate at which fruit rots.

When deciding on a location for your root cellar, take special care to ensure that any part of the finished structure that is directly exposed to the outside world never receives (or only minimally) direct sunlight. To maximize temperature control for future space, always build on the north side of a hill or in the shade.

Likewise, it is vital to ensure that any exposed parts of the root cellar will not be subject to rain runoff or leaks. Preventing such weather hazards is as simple as adding sloped doors or other drainage options but requires planning and foresight to attempt correctly.

Step 3: Root Cellar Placement

Before viewing root cellar designs, here are a few more things to consider when deciding where to place your root cellar for maximum efficiency and convenience. If you are planning to build your root cellar in your basement:

It may be easiest to provide two sides of the root cellar using the northeast corner of the house. After this, the other two sides can be filled in with board and stud.

Insulation is essential for keeping ambient house heat out.

The root cellar will still require its ventilation system.

If you intend to build your root cellar directly into the ground, scout the area for roots ahead of time; an abundance of roots will make digging the cellar more difficult and result in a less stable finished product.

Check for proper drainage. Sandy soil is ideal for this, as is building the cellar on a slope.

If the temperature in your area regularly falls below 25°F, ensure your cellar is dug deep enough to be below the frost line.

An easy alternative to modern insulation is straw and dried leaves; in cold climates, the dirt itself will not be enough.

Step 4: Materials

Tools:

- One or two long-handed shovels, plus a trench shovel for squaring off the hole you dig
- A hoe or something to spread concrete, plus a wooden float to smooth it
- A wheelbarrow
- Mortarboard, trowel, and jointer tool
- A level and a tape measure
- A plumb bob

- A hammer and a masonry chisel
- A saw to cut any lumber
- A keyhole saw for specialized cutting
- A plane for trimming rafters
- A set of screwdrivers and wrenches
- A caulking gun

Materials for the Floor:

- Stakes to mark off the area
- String
- Boards to establish the floor's perimeter
- Ready-mix concrete
- Materials for the walls:
- Hollow concrete blocks
- Masonry cement
- Wood

Note: You will be building a ceiling, a door with a frame, and a set of stairs. Ask a skilled employee at your local building supply store how much wood you'll need for your root cellar. Please be aware that all of the wood will need to be treated beforehand to prevent it from the high humidity levels in your root cellar.

Materials for Drainage and Ventilation:

- Drainage tiles
- Metal ventilation pipe, at least three feet long, plus a mesh screen to cover it
- Pipe covers to seal off ventilation when necessary

Additional Materials:

- A hatch door
- Spray foam insulation
- Extra weatherproofing for your doors
- Gravel

Step 5: Digging In

Note: Before you stab anything into the ground, you must first contact your local power supplier to check whether any power lines are buried in the ground.

You must first dig out or excavate a location for your root cellar. This can be done with a shovel or professional excavation equipment, depending on the size of the planned cellar and the soil. This is best done in early spring after the ground has thawed. If you need professional contractors to assist you with this project, you should hire them in early spring before their schedules fill up. However, before you dig, check the weather forecast; early spring rains could be disastrous.

When defining the dig area, leave more space around the perimeter than the actual floor area you intend to dig. For example, if your cellar is 8 feet by 8 feet, you should excavate a 10-foot by 10-foot section. This allows for the cellar walls and the soil that will be backfilled later.

The hole should be 4 feet deep to get your cellar below the frost line. Create a slope corresponding to the stairs on the side of the hole where you intend to put the entrance. You will almost certainly be constructing a doorway at the top and bottom of these stairs.

Be sure not to haul the soil you dig out too far away. You will be using it again.

Step 6: Foundations and Support Structures

Your root cellar needs a footing to be supported, especially after it has been fully stocked and covered with soil. It is strongly advisable that you speak with a concrete expert unless you have prior expertise pouring footings and foundations.

Stake out the surface area of your floor, then dig an even footing around the perimeter. This corresponds to the width of the walls and aids in weight distribution. You can then pour your footing. Allow the new concrete to harden for the required time before constructing the first level of mortar blocks on top of the footing to form the foundation of your wall.

However, you must first install your drainage tiles before building a wall. Pour two inches of gravel around the perimeter of the footing and slope it toward the door. Lay the tiles around the entire perimeter of the gravel bed, with the holes pointing downward. Drainage holes that are three feet wide and three feet deep should be located at the drainage tile's two ends that point toward the front of the structure. After that, cover the tiles with about a foot of extra gravel to support the weight of the backfilled soil.

The masonry blocks can be used to construct the supporting walls. If you've never constructed a brick wall before, get guidance from a professional or guide who can demonstrate how to cut the blocks so that the patterns change and your lines stay straight. It is probably a good idea to pour sawdust or another type of insulation down the holes before the final course of masonry blocks. Do this on the front wall, if not all of them.

When your walls are complete, it's time to install the roof. There are several possibilities for root cellar roofs, but keep in mind that once much of the structure has been covered with dirt, it will have to support a substantial load. Consult a roofing specialist to find out which designs can support the weight that your cellar will need, but generally speaking, you'll need strong support rafters and you'll need to build the roof at an angle that relieves pressure once the soil is on top. The advantage of building a cellar roof is that it only needs to be functional; no one will see it.

Note: If you are going to finish off your roof with concrete or tar, save that step for now. Ventilation will be covered shortly. Finish off the roof once you have figured out how to air your root cellar.

Step 7: An Entrance

Now that your doorway is in place, you must make entry and exit simple and convenient. First, construct a wall corresponding to the doorway and slope upward with the ground to accommodate the hatch door. Make sure to treat the wood you use to construct this wall. You'll need to build a small flight of stairs along the slope that leads to the doorway. You can get creative here but using a prefabricated set of stairs that line up with your doorway is the simplest option.

A hatch door may not be enough to keep the cold air out in colder climates. Consider fitting a second door into the frame you built in such cases. The most important thing, however, is to insulate the entrance. That is why you purchased spray foam insulation.

Line the hatch doorway's perimeter with spray foam insulation with care. It will start as a liquid but quickly expand into a thick, airtight foam. This type of insulation around doorways and joints is somewhat pricey, but it is well worth it because it effectively keeps air out.

Furthermore, insects or rodents certainly could not if air could not pass through those spaces. Your first line of defense against pests that can smell all the delicious food in your cellar will be this foam insulation.

Step 8: Ventilation

You now have a standing structure with a functional door and a nearly finished roof. It's time to build a ventilation pipe so that controlling temperature and humidity will be much easier in the future.

Start by making a hole in your roof between any two rafters with a keyhole saw that is the same width as your metal ventilation pipe. We recommended making this pipe at least three feet long so it can protrude well above the backfilled soil you will soon cover this cellar with. Pass the pipe through the hole you created and secure it tightly. More foam insulation is needed here to make the seam around the pipe waterproof.

At the top of the ventilation pipe, you'll need two covers: one conical in shape to keep out rain and heavy things, and one mesh screen attached over the entrance to keep out any insects or rodents that might fall down that pipe.

Finally, you need to create some kind of air-tight stopper for the cellar side of the ventilation pipe for airflow regulation. It would be adequate to use a straightforward rubber stopper that matches the pipe's aperture, but feel free to use something more elaborate.

Step 9: Electricity

Now is the right time to install any electricity if you choose and have been granted permission. Please note that the installation of electricity is an expert-only project. Unless you have extensive knowledge in installing electrical systems and running electricity lines, engage a professional to complete this task.

Step 10: Backfilling

It's time to bury your root cellar so it can benefit from the earth's temperature-regulating abilities. Remember all that soil you dug up to make room for your cellar? This is where it comes in handy. Backfilling the soil around your root cellar is as simple as using a shovel and a wheelbarrow. Make sure the cellar's structure is completely sealed, the roof is complete, and all the walls have hardened sufficiently to withstand the weight of all this soil.

Spread the first layer of soil around the perimeter with caution to avoid crushing the drainage tiles. Continue to build up around the perimeter until the soil reaches the height of the walls. Increase the soil around the entrance so that only the hatch door remains. After that, start mounding up the soil on the roof, taking care not to cover the ventilation pipe.

Once your root cellar is covered, seed or sod the soil and let grass begin to grow. You'll be prepared to start storing vegetables after a few weeks when it appears to have blended in organically with the surrounding landscape.

CHAPTER 6: ROOT CELLAR INTERIOR TIPS AND TRICKS FOR FURNITURE, STORAGE SPACE, AND UTILITIES

Once your root cellar has been set up, the actual effective operation of the cellar is pretty simple. It centers around keeping the humidity and the temperature from any severe fluctuations.

Lack of humidity can be countered by simply putting an open bucket of water in the corner if your cellar is too dry or sprinkling water on the floor.

If the cellar is too humid, increase the airflow and check that the interior is not troubled with water seepage and other wet problems.

Food Storage Shelves

You can build a food storage system with spare walls in your pantry or an extra room in your house. Fruit, some vegetables, and canned and dried foods can all be stored here as long as your shelves are kept in a dark, cool place.

You will later read step-by-step instructions for building shelving units.

Crawlspace

You can certainly convert your crawlspace, or a portion of it, into a storage room. Choose a location away from furnaces, water heaters, and other heat sources. Add sturdy shelving to make more space; if it has a dirt floor, that's even better because dirt floors are the best at regulating humidity. Although concrete floors are not ideal, they provide a longer lifespan for most vegetables. Bring out your creative side while keeping adequate ventilation in mind.

Plastic Tote

Plastic totes are an inexpensive way to extend the life of your root crops. All you have to do is partially bury the vegetables in sawdust, which will help with moisture regulation and keep the vegetables from touching each other. Using a tote, you can also keep your vegetables in the dark. This method works well for potatoes, beets, and carrots, and if you can't find sawdust, you can use a straw instead—while it will need to dry out, you can reuse sawdust or straw the following year.

Under Your Porch

You can use the space beneath your porch if you're exceptionally clever and inventive. A hole in the basement wall leading to the under-porch space is one design. The entrance is lined with rigid foam, which adds insulation from outside temperatures and is designed to blend in with the room from which it came.

These spaces are not large, but they can be used to store several pounds of potatoes or other root vegetables in an otherwise unutilized space.

Window Well in the Basement

If you don't have any extra space but have a basement window well, you can convert it into a mini-root cellar.

Your window well should ideally be on a north wall. Cover it with a layer of straw bales and orientated strand board (OSB). This keeps it cool but does not cause it to freeze. And if the bottom of your window well is layered with gravel, it will help regulate humidity levels.

You can stack milk crates to hold your vegetables; because these stacks well, you can make the most of your space. You can also hang dark curtains at the window to keep the light out.

This method of storing winter squash and potatoes works well. However, it is not suitable for those who are not mobile, as accessing it can be difficult.

Earth Pit

This was another popular method for storing root vegetables, similar to clamp storage. All you have to do is dig a shady and well-drained pit, ensuring that water drains away rather than into it.

Cover the bottom of the pit with sawdust or sand, then add your root vegetables and cover them with more sawdust or sand and a thick layer of straw or leaves. Weigh down a black plastic sheet with logs, rocks, bricks, or other heavy items.

Making Use of Cardboard Boxes

You can store your vegetables in cardboard boxes if you have space in a room or under your bed. The idea is straightforward: Put your vegetables in the box and cover them with something damp but not soaking wet. This gives the impression that your vegetables are resting beneath the ground, waiting to be picked.

You can use any size cardboard box appropriate for storing the vegetables. For most vegetables, the filling should be sand, peat moss, wood chips (make sure the wood chips are not toxic), or newspaper for potatoes.

Most vegetables do not need to be washed before storing; simply rub dirt off potatoes, but most other items can be stored dirty. They should be because the soil can help fight disease and protect the vegetables. Picking your vegetables or digging them up and placing them directly in the boxes is the best method.

All root vegetables should be trimmed to prevent deterioration and drying, leaving a couple of inches of top greenery on them.

For Potatoes:

1. Fill the bottoms of the boxes with newspaper sheets.
2. Dig up your potatoes, sort them into storage bags, and rub off the dirt. Take care not to harm the skin.
3. Sort your potatoes by size or variety and layer them in the bottom of the box in a single layer. Add another layer of newspaper, followed by another layer of potatoes. Repeat until the box is full.

For Additional Root Vegetables:

Apply a thin layer of filler material to the bottom of the box before adding your vegetables. Try to arrange them so that the carrots are horizontal and the turnips are upright. Place a layer of filler on top, followed by another layer of vegetables, and so on. Make sure the filler is moist—it will serve as a humidifier. Place the box in storage after closing it.

Check your vegetables regularly and discard any that are deteriorating or drying out. Beets are notorious for drying out quickly, but if you get to them quickly enough, you can still use them. Simply place them in a pan of simmering water to bring them back to life.

If you dry the filler out thoroughly, you can reuse it many times.

Organizing Your Space

How you design your space mainly depends on what you are storing. If you only keep one type of produce, ensure the humidity and temperature levels are even throughout the cellar.

Build shelves for the walls and other storage units using wood—they will not conduct the heat or cold the same way metal does and ensure the temperatures remain steady. Also, ensure your storage options are a couple of inches away from the walls to keep them dry. Using shelving means storing foods that need different temperatures, too—colder at the bottom, warmer at the top.

Lastly, load your products, and don't forget to check them weekly. Discard anything going bad and reap the rewards of all your hard work.

Your root cellar should be set up according to your preferences, financial constraints, tastes, and the items you want to store. Use old crates and boxes to set upon any shelves you design instead of purchasing many storage containers and filling them with sawdust or straw. Just remember to think vertically, *i.e.,* build-up. You won't be living in your cellar, so you should use as much space as possible for storage. Building tall shelves is one way to do this, which will then provide you freedom with humidity (remember, the area close to the ceiling will be warmer and more humid).

Storing Vegetables in Sand

You can do this with just about any container on hand and a supply of fine sand (the type used in kids' sandboxes).

Put a few inches of play sand and tuck in your root vegetables. You can also use this method for firm fruits like pears or apples. Cover with more sand, leaving space between the fruits/vegetables so they can breathe and the air circulate. You should leave about an inch between fruits.

Ensure you do not wash anything you store this way, which hastens the decomposition process. Simply brush the dirt off and cut off green bits, like carrot tops or beet greens.

Another way is to add sand to wooden or cardboard boxes and store them in basements, cellars, or even a garage—so long as it is not heated. It does not matter where as long as the temperature doesn't go below freezing.

The same procedure applies to the crisper drawer. Keep your fruits and vegetables separate, especially those that give off ethylene gas, such as apples. This gas speeds up ripening and can taint other vegetables and fruits. Store root vegetables vertically in the sand and the rest lying down.

In-Place Storage

There are several methods for in-place storage; just pick which one suits you.

Garden Rows

Carrots and beets will keep perfectly through the winter, and their flavor may even improve over time.

The idea is to insulate the rows against sub-zero temperatures. To accomplish this, poke holes in a black garbage bag and fill it with wet leaves. When ready to harvest your vegetables, simply place them over the top and lift them off. Harvest enough to last a few weeks, so you don't have to keep disturbing the rows and exposing them to the cold air. Furthermore, when spring arrives, those leaves are ideal for adding to your compost heap.

Another option is to remove the carrot tops. Freeze, bottle, or otherwise use the carrots. As insulation, the carrot tops can be piled on top of another row of vegetables. Then, cover it with black plastic and weigh it down with bricks.

Mounding

This is another technique. Several pockets are dug into the earth and vented to allow air to circulate. A drainage trench will direct water away from the pockets. The disadvantage is that all the food in a pocket must be harvested all at once, so it is best to make several small ones. The pockets are insulated with straw and dirt layers, and this method works for onions, potatoes, and any other food that needs to be stored in dry conditions.

Hay Bale Storage

This necessitates constructing a hay bale structure around your vegetable rows. This is finished with a large sheet of plexiglass or a recycled storm door, transforming it into a cold frame. A blanket or tarp can be used for extra insulation in freezing weather. This method allows you to harvest food as needed rather than all at once, and it works well with crops that prefer moist conditions, such as carrots, winter radishes, and beets.

Mini Hoop-Houses

The final method involves building mini hoop-houses over your rows. These are made from lengths of PVC piping and clear plastic sheeting. You can find many different ways of doing this online, and they are pretty easy to construct and allow your crops to be harvested as you want them.

Basic Tips

All households have different eating habits, and the design and contents of all root cellars will vary wildly depending on the household's needs. For most people, root cellars offer a great place to store root vegetables and tubers, such as carrots, potatoes, parsnips, beets, and so on.

You might ask why you cannot just go and buy these as you need them. Well, you can if you want; however, take a careful look at the quality of the vegetables in your grocery store. They are often damaged and bruised; some already go off and are generally tasteless.

As such, these are the basic principles you must follow to successfully plan and build your root cellar.

- **Check with Your Local Building Department**: The last thing you want is to violate any building codes. Before you start building your root cellar, check with your local building department to see if there are any requirements or regulations you must follow. Before you begin, you must follow all construction or building codes that apply to your project and ensure you have all the necessary permits.

- **Make a Plan**: Design your root cellar to meet your food storage needs, considering any physical limitations you may have. For example, if you have difficulty using a ladder or stairs, choose a more accessible root cellar design.

- **Choose Your Size**: Your root cellar must be large enough to hold all your food. For example, if you grow an acre of food, building a tiny root cellar that can only hold a fraction of what you harvest is pointless. If you only have a small amount to store, don't build a massive one. If you build underground, keep the following safety precautions in mind. Some potential hazards include structural failure, accumulated unwanted gases, cave-ins, etc. So, build your cellar from the ground up, ensuring it's safe, sound, and has enough ventilation.

- **Consider the Location**: You must consider every aspect of the land where you intend to build your root cellar. Some areas have extremely high water tables, while others have septic systems, which can be disastrous because the root cellar will flood and fail.

- **Consider the Critical Aspects**: When designing, consider controlling temperature, drainage, ventilation, and humidity. These factors are significant and will influence how long your food will last in storage. People frequently approach building a root cellar based on the type of food they intend to store. So, as you create your plan, ask yourself the following questions:

- **The Foundations**: Next, you must plan the foundations of your cellar. You must dig a minimum of ten feet to reach the ground level, where the temperature stabilizes.

- **Lining the Walls**: If possible, use cinder blocks— they are less expensive, more malleable, and excellent for lining your walls. Remember that your walls must be built on the foundation to ensure their stability; you'd be surprised at how many people put in the floor first, then build their walls to the sides!

- **Plan Your Floor**: While many believe pouring a cement floor is the best option, the best flooring for a root cellar is gravel and natural dirt. This works better than a concrete floor at retaining moisture. The goal is to maintain a high humidity level; the more moisture you can keep, the better.

- **The Roof**: Graded ceilings are far superior for keeping rain and other external elements out and preventing them from resting on the cellar roof. Heavy rain or snow piled on the roof can add significant weight, all of which bears down on your cellar foundations.

- **Ventilation**: This is important in constructing your root cellar because it prevents too much humidity and moisture from spoiling your crops. Excess moisture causes condensation, which, as you are aware, results in water running everywhere, causing your crops to rot and spoil.

If you want to convert an existing building or space, ensure you follow the same guidelines for location and make the right alterations to fit what you want.

CHAPTER 7: HARVESTING, STORING, TRACKING, AND PLANNING

Beets

Beets should be harvested after a few days of dry weather if the roots have a diameter of around 2 inches. Dig up the beets, remove the greens, leaving 1 to 2 inches on the root, and brush off the loose soil.

The beets should not be washed. Simply place them in a lidded bucket or a wooden box filled with damp sand, peat moss, or sawdust. Make sure your beets are not touching. If you're using a bucket, put the lid on to help retain moisture, but don't tighten it (you still need air circulation).

Check on your beets from time to time and remove any that appear to be going bad—like apples, one bad beet can ruin the lot.

Varieties:

The following varieties are ideal for long-term storage:

- Long Season
- Boltardy
- Lutz Green Leaf

Shelf Life: Beets will store anywhere between three and five months.

Broccoli

Broccoli is not well known for being a long-storage vegetable. You can make it last for a couple of weeks when stored correctly.

Dig up your broccoli and trim the stems. You can store it in perforated plastic bags or hang it upside down in the cellar. However you do it, ensure you do not store it near any fruit, such as apples, that releases ethylene gas, as this can dramatically shorten its storage life.

Varieties:

The following varieties are ideal for long-term storage:

- Green Comet
- Greenbelt
- Marathon
- Legacy
- Waltham 29

Shelf Life: Between one and two weeks at most.

Brussels Sprouts

Brussels sprouts, whether you like them or not, are good for storing—though they do not have a long shelf life. Before harvesting your sprouts for the best flavor, wait until several touches of frost have passed. If you have enough space in your cellar, carefully dig up the plant and plant it in a container. Place it in your cellar and continue to harvest it. Alternatively, hang it by the roots in the cellar. Harvest your sprouts and store them in perforated plastic bags if you don't have much space.

Varieties:

The following varieties are ideal for long-term storage:

- Long Island Improved
- Jade Cross

Shelf Life: Between three and five weeks.

Cabbage

Red cabbage varieties will store better than their green or white counterparts, and late varieties are better than early ones.

Harvest your cabbages when the first frost has passed. Pull or dig the plant up and trim the leaves off. Choose cabbages with solid, unblemished heads to store.

These are best stored in bins or outside pits—if you store them indoors, the cabbage odor will go right through the cellar or house and can severely impact how pears, apples, and celery taste. If you can only store them in the root cellar, each head should be wrapped in paper and stored on a shelf, with a few inches between each one.

Varieties:

The following varieties are ideal for long-term storage:

- Danish Ballhead
- Brunswick
- Red Acre
- Late Flat Dutch
- Storage No 4
- Red Drumhead

Shelf Life: Between three and four months, depending on the variety.

Carrots

Carrots are one of the best root crops for storing right in the garden, but only if you don't have any pest problems and can mulch the carrots with one to two feet of straw or hay.

If you need to store them indoors, harvest them before the ground freezes at the end of the season. Cut or snap the tops off as close to the carrot as possible, leaving just a tiny bit. Leaving too much green on the carrot will deplete its nutrients and moisture and will not last long.

Lay the carrots in peat, moss, or damp sandboxes.

Varieties:

The following varieties are ideal for long-term storage:

- Danvers
- Kingston
- Chantenay
- Carson
- Bolero
- Nigel
- Kurota Chantenay
- Royal Chantenay
- Red Core Chantenay
- St Valery

Shelf Life: Between four and six months, depending on the variety and storage conditions.

Jerusalem Artichokes

Jerusalem artichokes keep better in the ground than root cellars, lasting the entire winter if not frozen. If you choose to leave them in the ground, you must take precautions because frost and freezing temperatures will break down the starches. Their texture, color, and flavors will change, and any diseased or bruised will spoil quickly.

Dig them up, remove the tops, and brush off the soil if you want to store them in your root cellar. They should be kept in plastic bags or damp sand in containers. They should not be stored in places where they will dry out and shrivel, as they do not store as well as potatoes.

Varieties:

The following varieties are ideal for long-term storage:

- Fuseau (most common)
- Coris Bolton Haynes (less common)

Shelf Life: All winter in the ground, provided the ground does not freeze. Suppose stored in the root cellar for up to ten days in plastic bags and one to two months in the sand.

Leeks

Leeks are another vegetable that can survive in the ground over the winter or until the first hard frost. Mulch your leeks heavily and keep them that way until after the frost. Dig them up, making sure their roots stay intact.

Fill a deep bucket with soil or damp sand and plant the leeks upright.

Varieties:

The following varieties are ideal for long-term storage:

- Musselburgh
- Arena
- Elephant
- Nebraska
- Zermatt

Shelf Life: Between three and four months in the cellar, all winter in the ground, provided you do not get frost.

Parsnips

Parsnips, like carrots, can be left to grow in the ground over the winter. Cover them with thick mulch and harvest them as needed. However, parsnips dislike freeze/thaw cycles and should be harvested if your winters are cold.

Cut off the tops at the end of the season, before or just after the first frost. Store in sphagnum moss, damp sand, or peat-layered boxes.

Varieties:

The following varieties are ideal for long-term storage:

- Hollow Crown
- All-America
- Offenham

Shelf Life: Between one and two months.

Pears

Pears are incredibly sensitive to changes in temperature and should be stored at the lower end of 29-31°F. If you store them at higher temperatures or for too long, the pears do not ripen. Instead, they break down, turning brown and mushy inside while the outside still looks fine.

Like apples, you should store only the unbruised and unblemished fruits, preferably with their stems. Each pear should be wrapped in a paper bag or newspaper and stored in wooden or cardboard boxes with a perforated plastic lining. This allows air circulation while keeping moisture levels up.

Varieties:

The following varieties are ideal for long-term storage:

- D'anjou
- Comice
- Bosc

Shelf Life: Between two and three months.

Potatoes

Unsurprisingly, potatoes are one of the best root vegetables to store in a root cellar, given that they were the original reason root cellars were built.

Wait until the foliage has died before replanting the potatoes for another two weeks—this aids in the curing and hardening of the skin for storage. Sort through your potatoes after carefully digging them up.

Set aside any bruised or damaged potatoes to be used right away. If any of them have green spots, don't eat them because green is a chemical that can cause digestive and intestinal upset.

Sort the potatoes by size; keep the same-sized potatoes together and brush off any dirt. They should not be washed. Place the potatoes in a dark place at 45 to 60°F for ten to fourteen days to cure.

After that, the potatoes can be stored in bins, boxes, or burlap sacks. Shredded paper should be placed between each layer of potatoes in boxes or bins, and air holes should be cut into the sides.

Do not store potatoes near any fruits that give off ethylene; do not allow the temperature to rise, as this will prompt the potatoes to start sprouting.

Varieties:

Most late potato varieties will store just fine (early and second early varieties are not meant for storage). The following varieties are ideal for long-term storage:

- All Blue
- Red Pontiac
- Kennebec
- Sangre
- Katahdin
- Yukon Gold

- Sebago

Shelf Life: Between four and six months.

Rutabagas

Like most root vegetables, Rutabagas can survive the winter in the ground. To keep the ground from freezing, apply a layer of mulch 10 to 12 inches thick, extending it about 18 inches on either side of the row. Even if there is a couple of feet of snow, the roots are safe. They must be harvested before the spring, or else new growth will sprout from the tops.

If you can't leave them in the ground all winter, lift them at the end of the growing season, brush off the dirt, and twist off the tops to store them for longer. You should not wash them, but if you do, they must be completely dry before being stored.

Sort through the roots and set aside any damaged ones; these cannot be stored and must be consumed immediately.

Layer the good roots in a wooden box or bucket with sawdust, peat moss, or damp sand. The roots should be packed and covered but not touching one another, and the container should not be completely sealed to allow the moist air to circulate.

Varieties:

The following varieties are ideal for long-term storage:

- Laurentian
- American Purple Top

Shelf Life: Between two and six months, depending on the variety.

Turnips

These should be treated the same as carrots and kept moist. However, unlike carrots, turnips should be stored in an outdoor pit if possible. Otherwise, the smell permeates and taints the flavors of other foods.

Varieties:

The following varieties are ideal for long-term storage:

- Purple White Top Globe
- Navet des Vertus Marteau

Shelf Life: Between four and six months.

Winter Radishes

Winter radishes can withstand temperatures as low as 28°F and can be left in the ground if heavily mulched. However, if you must store them away from the ground, consider an outdoor ground pit or garbage bins, as they emit a strong odor indoors.

If you're storing them in a root cellar, cut the tops off, leaving an inch of stem, and layer them with sphagnum moss or sand in boxes or baskets.

Varieties:

The following varieties are ideal for long-term storage:

- Chinese White
- Black Spanish
- Violet de Gournay

Shelf Life: Between two and three months.

Onions

Lift the onions when the tops turn brown and fall. Dig them up during a dry day and spread them on hardware cloth, a screen, or a newspaper. Let them sit somewhere cool, dark, and well-ventilated for ten to fourteen days or until the roots have dried and the skin has turned papery.

Cut the tops off, leaving about an inch, and store them in paper bags, net bags, or even pantyhose. Do not use plastic containers or bags that are not breathable—if onions are not stored in dry conditions, they will begin sprouting.

Varieties:

The following varieties are ideal for long-term storage:

- Brunswick
- Australian Brown
- Copra
- Red Burgundy
- Bronze d'Amposta
- Newburg
- Red Creole
- Norstar
- Red Weathersfield
- Stuttgarter
- Rossa di Milano
- Yellow of Parma
- Yellow Globe

- Sweet varieties do not store very well.

Shelf Life: Between five and eight months.

Pumpkins

Pumpkins should be harvested before the first frost because they dislike cold weather and will be killed by frost. Leave about an inch of stem on the pumpkin to prevent spoilage.

Allow them to cure for about ten days at 80 to 85 degrees. You can leave them outside if the weather is warm and dry. The curing process hardens the skins, allowing them to be stored for a longer period. However, any bruised, damaged, or broken stems should not be stored.

The pumpkins can then be piled up in your root cellar, two or three deep, so long as they are in a dry area—off the floor may be best.

Varieties:

The following varieties are ideal for long-term storage:

- Winter Luxury
- Howdens

Shelf Life: Between five and six months.

Sweet Potatoes

Sweet potatoes should be harvested as soon as the vines have died, usually in late fall. Dig the potatoes carefully, putting damaged tubers to one side for immediate consumption. Brush the loose soil from undamaged tubers and cure them for five to ten days, at a temperature of 80-85°F and with 90% humidity.

After this time, you can move them into the root cellar, wrapping each tuber in paper and layering them in ventilated baskets or boxes.

Varieties:

The following varieties are ideal for long-term storage:

- Centennial
- Allgold
- Jewell

Shelf Life: Between four and six months.

Tomatoes

You are not required to wait for your tomatoes to ripen on the vine. You can pick them while they are still green and allow them to mature in storage, or choose varieties better suited to longer storage. Some tomatoes store much better than others if the conditions are favorable.

If you're storing green tomatoes, pull the entire vine from the ground and hang it upside down in the cellar. Alternatively, you can select the tomatoes and individually wrap each one in the paper. Store them at around 55°F to allow them to ripen slowly; do not store them below this temperature, or they will not ripen. Green tomatoes typically take ten to fourteen days to ripen at the ideal temperature.

Varieties:

The following varieties are ideal for long-term storage:

- Eva Purple Ball
- Green Thumb
- Fried Green Hybrid
- Old Fashioned Garen Peach

- Reverend Morrow's Long Keeper
- Red Siberian
- Red October
- Winter Keeper
- Ruby Treasure

Shelf Life: Between one and two months for standard green tomatoes; up to six months for long storage varieties.

CHAPTER 8: YEARLY MAINTENANCE (TIPS, TRICKS, MUST DO, LOG PLAN, CHECKLIST)

Cleaning and Sanitizing a Root Cellar

The last thing worth discussing is cleaning your root cellar. This should be done twice a year, the first time in March or April and the second before storing your next harvest.

Most of your remaining root crops will have passed their best storage limits by the spring. Whatever you didn't use must be consumed or discarded, depending on whether it's good or bad. While potatoes, garlic, and onions are probably still safe, you should eat them soon or plant them in the garden to produce a new crop.

If you have an abundance of good vegetables that you cannot use immediately, find another way to store them. A lovely pan of scalloped potatoes can be made with potatoes, garlic, and onion! Make a batch of meals with your vegetables that you can freeze for another day.

If you have vegetables that can be stored for a few months, remove them from the cellar. While doing your spring cleaning, keep them in burlap sacks or dark, ventilated containers. They won't be exposed to light, and the air will still circulate, keeping them fresh. Set aside canned and bottled foods.

Remove any storage bins, crates, and boxes once you've cleared out all of your food from the cellar. Cardboard boxes may be usable for another year; if not, throw them away. It is best to burn them if they have bacteria or mold growth spots.

Reusable containers should be scrubbed out thoroughly. Use a weak bleach solution to kill bacteria and wash them in boiling water. Leave them to dry naturally.

Back into the root cellar, give it a good sweep. Clear up any dust, dirt, and debris from the shelves and the floor.

Once your root cellar is cleared out, leave the doors open to air out for a few days. If the cellar still smells musty, run a fan there for a few days to help evacuate the stale air.

Before you store your next harvest in the autumn, go back in there, have a final sweep out, rewash your storage containers and close down your vents. You do not want the warmer summer air getting in. Now you are ready to start over.

As a side note, you can use your root cellar in the summer months to keep early fruits and vegetables cool when you don't have time to process them straight away. However, do not leave them there for more than a few days.

During spring cleaning, go through your root cellar and list any repairs, improvements, or upgrades needed. Check for rot or damage if you use wood in any structures; this must be replaced first.

Examine the seals around your ventilation pipes and replace them as needed. Do the same with doors and windows, and make sure any drainage issues are addressed immediately.

Make sure you have enough storage containers and bags—buy new ones if necessary. Check that your old ones are in good shape, with no nails or loose bits protruding.

Check that your ventilation covers are in place and replace them if necessary. When the temperature outside is low enough, open your vent covers.

While root cellars are relatively easy to maintain, you need to be on top of monitoring it, especially when yours is newly built at the start of the season. Two of the most important things you can invest in are a hygrometer and a thermometer. As established, you must maintain the following conditions in your cellar:

- Humidity — 90-95%
- Temperature — 32-40°F
- Ventilation — Constant and adequately installed

Keeping the temperature stable is possibly the hardest thing to do. Most root cellars rely on the soil temperature to keep the cellar cool. Based on your climate, you may need to consider digging your cellar in a bit deeper—this is why research is critical.

It is relatively simple to raise humidity levels—leave a few water bowls in the cellar. Then, experiment with humidity and see how many bowls you need to use to get the humidity at the right level. However, be mindful of ensuring your root cellar is secured; water can attract insects and other unwelcome creatures.

By contrast, if you need to lower the humidity level, make your ventilation a bit bigger or angle it to where the winds prevail from in your region. Ensure your ventilation is covered with a screen; otherwise, you will get insects, dirt, rain, and all sorts in your cellar.

Adequate ventilation will stop ethylene gas from building up and destroying your food or causing it to sprout too early. Ethylene is odorless and is typically associated with fruits like bananas and apples.

Canned and Bottled Foods

Anything stored in jars, bottles, or otherwise preserved must be handled differently. When you began with your root cellar, you should have started a notebook detailing the dates each item was preserved and placed into storage. You should also have labeled each container with the date of preservation.

Your first job is to go through everything. Check for anything that has expired or gone off, and discard it in the garbage. Go by the dates on your containers or in your notebook—the earliest products should have been used first, so all you should have in storage are those stored later. However, if your system went awry, you may be left with old food—you really should not eat this unless it has been pickled. Dairy products are way past their "best by" date by now unless they have only just been placed into storage.

Also, dispose of any rusted, dented, or bulging cans and foods with torn or broken packaging.

Now, you can deal with what is left.

Wipe down all jars, cans, bottles, etc., to eliminate any dirt, dust, or sticky residue.

Restock your cellar using a FIFO system—First In, First Out. The older stuff should be used first, or it will go off soon.

CONCLUSION

Thank you for reading this book. Once your root cellar is up and running, take a moment to reflect on how far you've come. Then, in January, take a big bite of one of your vegetables, either from the farmers' market or your garden. Consider the tasteless produce grown on other continents and now available on the shelves of your local supermarket. The difference will be enormous. You currently possess a vegetable that tastes exactly as it should, a flavor that many of us have forgotten, in your root cellar.

Root vegetables like potatoes, carrots, parsnips, beets, and turnips are ideal for this type of storage because root cellars were originally intended to store them. People store much more, such as apples, flower bulbs, canned goods, pears, pickled vegetables, etc. Consider a root cellar to be a large extension of your pantry.

Root cellars use the earth to keep humidity, light, and temperature levels stable. The ideal temperature range is 32-40°F, and the ideal humidity range is 85-95%. A successful root cellar requires humidity, darkness, and good ventilation.

The temperature is critical. Temperature management enables the gradual release of ethylene gas from fruits and vegetables, which promotes the growth of microorganisms and slows the decomposition process. High humidity, on the other hand, prevents moisture from evaporating.

Good luck.

Made in United States
Troutdale, OR
06/17/2024